BRED ANY GOOD ROOKS LATELY?

Bred any good rooks lately?

A collection of
puns, shaggy dogs, spoonerisms,
feghoots & malappropriate stories

GATHERED BY
JAMES CHARLTON

ILLUSTRATED BY MARY KORNBLUM

DOUBLEDAY & COMPANY, INC.
GARDEN CITY, NEW YORK
1986

Library of Congress Cataloging-in-Publication Data

Bred any good rooks lately?

1. American wit and humor. 2. Puns and punning. 3. Spoonerisms.

I. Charlton, James   1939-

PN6162.B697   1986   817'.54'08   86-4607
                ISBN 0-385-23477-5 (pbk.)

ACKNOWLEDGMENTS

I want to thank the writers who contributed to this volume and the many others who wrote a post card or letter of support. My appreciation to Steve King for letting me use his punchline for the title and to Walter Redfern for his awesome book on puns. My thanks and love to Barbara Binswanger, who put up with at least a year of punning, thanks to Danielle Grado for her editorial help, and to Mary Kornblum for her skill and creativity. And finally, my gratitude to my editor, Nick Bakalar, who had enough faith in *Bred Any Good Rooks Lately?* to make an offer first at William Morrow and then at Doubleday.

CONTENTS

*L*et's get it out of the way right up front—puns are *not* the lowest form of humor. Puns, deliberate spoonerisms and malaprops are a special kind of word play practiced and appreciated by nimble minds and fast wits. Even if the pun *were* the lowest form of humor it would still be, as Henry Erskine observed, "the foundation of all wit."

And not all puns are bad puns. "Puns are good, bad or indifferent," Fowler observed, and automatically describing *a pun* as *a bad pun* "is a sign at once of sheepish docility and desire to seem superior." Certainly the contributors here would heartily agree.

Puns have always been the stepchildren of humor, tolerated, but rarely presented as their parents' pride and joy. They have been called many things—catches, clinches, quibbles, among others—but rarely given their due. Yet puns communicate. "The pun demands a close collaboration between reader and author, listener and speaker," as Walter Redfern wrote. They demand of the reader a background of sophistication. A clever play on a word or a phrase without an intelligent receiver is a seed fallen on barren ground. It leaves the punner and the listener feeling foolish.

Foolishness was not something I had in mind when I asked a number of authors to write a story ending with a malaproped quotation or popular phrase. I gave them sample endings (which they all blithely ignored) and got in return some of the cleverest short stories ever gathered together. The stories rarely take the form of a simple pun, a play on words that comes out of the blue and has no setup. For the most part the clues to all the endings are contained in the stories. In a few cases, especially with the better-known punchlines, it's difficult to hide the verbal clues and the reader knows where the author is going. But the ride is a pleasure nonetheless.

Now exactly what are we to call these stories? Surely the broad umbrella is the pun, but the stories take many forms. Some are paragrams, a play on words altering one or more letters. "Assonant puns" these are called by Hughes and Hammond in their book *Upon the Pun*. Other stories rely on synonyms (different words with the same meaning) or homonyms (same word with different meanings). Rarer than the homonym is the animal called the heteronym (same spelling, different sound) which makes its appearance in several of the contributions. And the homophonic story, as practiced by oppenheimer and others, uses soundalike words with different meanings (actually joel oppenheimer throws in a homonymic knuckleball as well). So to call the stories "puns" is to ignore their many dimensions.

Nor are these "shaggy dogs," those interminable stories that spiral downward to a flat punchline—"oh, he's not so hairy" is the example given in many dictionaries—although they occasionally bear some resemblance to their hairy cousin. A good case can be made for calling them "feghoots." This was a term I was not familiar with before starting this book, but several writers admonished me for referring to these stories by any other name. Ferdinand Feghoot is the main character in hundreds of very short science-fiction stories written over the past decades under the pen name Grendal Briarton. Since all the stories have setups and end with a pun, the form could very appropriately be called a "feghoot." Grendal Briarton, the *nom de calembour* of Reginald Bretnor, has written a delightful story included in this collection. And several other writers, in homage to his wit and diligence, have used the term in their story or title.

"The reader's eye not only prefers one sound, one tone, in isolation, it prefers one meaning at a time. Puns—like ambiguities—the life of spoken discourse—become, in writing, affronts to taste, floutings of efficiency."

Thus spake Marshall McCluhan, who was correct when he wrote that the reader's eye prefers one meaning at a time. Many of these stories depend on being read aloud. There are a few stories which are, in fact, written puns, many which work either way, and several which are determinedly audible. A number of readers, several of whom are contributors, missed endings until they were read aloud and in several cases, spoken in a certain rhythm. With this book, referring to the appendix for the answer is not cheating; you are in very good company.

As far as "affronts to taste" are concerned, many of the contributors (and, we trust, readers) of *Bred Any Good Rooks Lately?* would gleefully concur. Bad taste abounds. But Marshall, these are some of the best writers in the land, playing with words, verbally juggling, rolling their sleeves up to show no hidden cards and then pulling a joker out of your ear.

I hope every reader is taken in, smitten with the range of these stories. The list of authors who stooped to pen these contributions is astonishing; at the risk of making a *Montaigne* out of a molehill, rarely has a collection of original stories included such a panoply of talent. To all those writers, poets and friends, my thanks. The firm conviction they all share that they have made a significant contribution to Western Literature should sustain them at least through the reviews.

Jim Charlton
New York City

BRED ANY GOOD ROOKS LATELY?

For the Birds

STEPHEN KING

Okay, this is a science-fiction joke.

It seems like in 1995 or so the pollution in the atmosphere of London has started to kill off all the rooks. And the city government is very concerned because the rooks roosting on the cornices and the odd little crannies of the public buildings are a big attraction. The Yanks with their Kodaks, if you get it. So they say, "What are we going to do?"

They get a lot of brochures from places with climates similar to London's so they can raise the rooks until the pollution problem is finally licked. One place with a similar climate, but low pollution count, turns out to be Bangor, Maine. So they put an ad in the paper soliciting bird fanciers and talk to a bunch of guys in the trade. Finally, they engage this one guy at the rate of $50,000 a year to raise rooks. They send an ornithologist over on the Concorde with two cases of rook eggs packed in these shatterproof cases — they keep the shipping compartment constantly heated and all that stuff.

So this guy has a new business—North American Rook Farms, Inc. He goes to work right off incubating new rooks so London will not become a rookless city. The only thing is, the London City Council is really impatient, and every day they send him a telegram that says: *"Bred Any Good Rooks Lately?"*

Rook to King

DONALD HALL

*A*ctually, Stephen King has it mixed up.

Here where we live in New Hampshire, the little creeks roll down Ragged Mountain across our fields, squirt under Route 4, and piddle into our hayfields on the other side. My wife spends all fall and much of the spring working on borders to these little springs, planting bulbs, fertilizing, and then keeping the borders clear and clean, because if there's anything she likes, it's to *weed a good brook*.

The Lad Is Not for Burning

JOHN D. MACDONALD

One of the great unsung heroes of the American West in the third and fourth decades of the nineteenth century was a Jewish frontiersman named Moses Noss. He was a mountain man, scout, trapper and Indian fighter, roaming the wild country in all seasons accompanied only by his Irish cook and companion, McNulty.

On one hot and windy September afternoon in the flatlands of what is now called Oklahoma, a roving plundering tribe of Plains Indians overtook Noss and McNulty out in the open. While Noss engaged the warriors with his skill and fabulous strength and agility, McNulty escaped. The Indians took Moses Noss back to their temporary village, erected a stake in the middle of the circle of wigwams, tied the mountain man to it, piled brush around his legs, and began the long afternoon of dancing and drum thumping and yelping, preparing to light the brush when it was full dark.

McNulty had tracked the captors and he hid in a nearby ravine until dusk. Then, slowly and carefully, he crept to the long line of tethered horses and silently freed all of them. He sent them off into the night, all of them except one giant red stallion. At precisely the right moment he came galloping into the village astride the horse, firing left and right. As the braves took cover he slashed the bonds of the captive and swung him onto the horse, and they thundered off into the night, safe to continue with their legendary deeds.

To this day descendants of that tribe shake their heads sadly and sigh, *"A stolen roan gathered Moe Noss."*

Gospel Rap

ROY BLOUNT JR.

*F*ella saw a woman coming down the street,
She looked so good he was indiscreet—
Said, "Hey there, Mama, you're a mover.
If that ain't so, I'm Herbert Hoover."

"Mm-Mm," she said.

He said, "I swear,
You got such sweet long legs and hair.
I doubt I've seen the likes of you."

"Well," she said, "that may be true."

"Hey," he said, "I've got some sheer
Long fine black silk stockings here.
I'd like to help you slip them on."

"Whoa," she said, "you hold the phone.
We got to talk about—you know—religion."

"What's that got to do with it, Pigeon?"

"*Ev*-ry-thing for a girl like me."

"Well," he said, right casually,
"I recognize *no* higher power.
Our . . . *acquaintance* has gone sour."

She said, "Your legwear may be great,
But listen here while I quotate
(As she stepped off on her heels and toes):
" '*There are no foxes in atheists' hose.*' "

A Day with Sam Goldwyn

WILLIAM EASTLAKE

My first trip to Hollywood was a job at the Samuel Goldwyn Studios, where Sam told me, "We're making an up-tic pic about the Jewish soldiers in Vietnam who were self-conscious about eating their Passover food in front of the goyim, so they ate it at night when they were dug in. You got a title for us?"

"Yes," I said. *"There Are No Atheists in Lox Holes."*

While we were sitting in the back of Sam's Mercedes, we were watching one of his old pictures on the telly. I told him that since the breakup of the big studios, Hollywood, with its emphasis on the new, rough realism, didn't seem able to make good pictures any more. Sam agreed. "It's true," he said. "In the old days we didn't shoot our pictures in dirty alleys, but always used upscale interiors. Even if the lady star was supposed to be working in a five-and-dime, when Clark Gable visited Jean Harlow she lived like a queen because we spent millions on interior shots. The sets all had handmade furniture, imported lamps and the latest expensive appliances. It's sad but true," Sam said as he let me out at my hotel. *"Hollywood doesn't make good fixtures any more."*

Lupe Has the Last Word

GEORGE GARRETT

"*H*ey!" Hector's wife Lupe always used to say, back in the early days when he was playing in the minors and couldn't get shoes big enough to fit him. "*If you can't stand on the feet, get out of the pitching!*" Sure, you remember Hector Espanola, the Tex-Mex with the blazing fastball and plenty of junk, too, in his repertoire. Five times a twenty-game winner; pitched a shutout in the Series; nine consecutive strikeouts in a Red Sox game; Hall of Fame just a few years ago.

But, like everybody else, you probably don't know that he never got shoes until he went up to the Yankees. He would complain about it all the time and Lupe would nag at him for being such a whiner. "Nag, nag, nag," he said (who had never heard of Sam Goldwyn). "Criticism rolls off my back like a duck."

People have forgotten, too, all the trouble he had with those Urdu brothers, the rowdy Finnish twins who played in the outfield for Waco. Somehow they could hit everything he had, and they damn near kept him in the minors forever with them. Hector had no alternative but to dust them off and knock them down every time they stepped up to the plate. They had no honorable choice but to go after him, aiming for the big head of the bare feet with their bats. Plenty of bad feeling all around.

When he was called up to the majors, they hooted and jeered and made bad Bronx cheers in the newspapers. But years later, when he made the Hall of Fame, they swallowed their anger and pride and sent him their warm and hearty congratulations. "Well, we've passed a lot of water under the bridge since then," Hector opined, showing Lupe their telegram.

"Hey," she cried (who never heard of Leo Durocher). "*Finnish guys nice at last!*"

Hyacinth and Fern

ANNE BERNAYS

*I*t seems that after years of homelessness the Salamander Athletic Club, a track-and-field team, finally had a grand new home all its own just outside Memphis, Tennessee.

Everybody in town was anxious to tour the new facility; it was rumored to have the very latest in training equipment— Nautilus, whirlpool, a banked track and the like—all, of course, scaled to salamander size.

The place was magnificent in every way, from the landscaping outside—hyacinth and fern—to the two dozen showers, each fitted with an adjustable spray head. The club— known as SAC—rapidly took in so many new members that for the first time in its history it had a waiting list. The Board of Governors hired the most accomplished trainers and coaches they could find, for the membership was determined not only to compete in national and international events but to win!

SAC's V.P. in charge of P.R. took daily visitors around SAC headquarters to observe the salamanders busily swimming back and forth in their Olympic-size pool, lifting weights and practicing the broad jump. Visitors were encouraged to ask questions.

"What are you doing there?" a thick-headed fellow asked Tim, one of the running coaches, although it was perfectly obvious to everyone else that the five small creatures in front of them, lined up and bent double, were about to run the fifty-yard dash.

The coach was a polite and patient individual, however, and answered without a trace of scorn, *"Why, I'm trying to find all the newts that's fit to sprint."*

The Tuchbreider Marriage

STEPHEN BIRMINGHAM

*A*fter seventeen and a half years, the thrill had gone out of LeRoy and Beryl Tuchbreider's marriage. It was LeRoy Tuchbreider's suggestion that possibly some new romance could be injected into the relationship if they were to try some novel and exotic positions in their lovemaking. But experiment after experiment was unsuccessful. In one endeavor, involving the donning of beachwear by the pair, the only result was that a brand-new pair of Beryl Tuchbreider's terrycloth beach pajamas from Saks was torn to shreds. Discouraged, the couple decided to seek professional advice from a marriage counselor.

"Describe to me exactly the various lovemaking positions you have tried," the counselor said. When the Tuchbreiders came to the end of their litany, the counselor shook his head and said, "Each of those positions is wrong, wrong, *wrong*." Citing the incident with the new beach pajamas from Saks, the counselor added that this was a perfect example of the well-known maxim that *"It's a wrong lay to rip a terry."*

Just Rewards

ELIZABETH TALLENT

*I*n a tiny, remote, greener-than-green county in England there was a castle named Justwanna. The castle had been abandoned by its most recent human inheritor to its rightful (by virtue of vindictive tenacity) owners, a pair of ghosts. The curious thing is that these ghouls were female, twins who had fallen in love—in 1643 or so—with the same young lord. After attempting literally to divide him, one twin with an intaglio dagger and the other with her father's sword—which hung, still sheeny and perceptibly haunted, over the library mantelpiece—the twins were executed, but though thoroughly dead for centuries they had never quite left home.

In the rather more depressed and unenergetic year 1985, the young Lord of Foon had been sainted in certain smudgy, sly working-class tabloids for his love life, which was the most interesting thing going on in England. His looks were aristocratically remote and his lovers were, to the paper's delight, many, photogenic, and even now and then, American. (There was an adventure with an African but this was hushed up, though she went on to become a singing star). The young Lord Foon was induced by the company that wished to open Justwanna as a stop on a lucrative package tour for Americans, a kind of pricey bed-and-croissant place in which the trusting travelers were assured they would encounter only noble ghosts, to tour the ninety-four recently redone rooms, to lie rakishly across a satin bed here, and lean a jaunty elbow against a mantelpiece there. It was considered that Foon by his very appearance would escalate the tour's bookings into the pleasantest prospect for success. Foon kissed his newest lady love—a TV detective—goodbye, and climbed into his tiny, purring MG in the pattering London rain.

It was with sinking hearts and hastily lowered teacups that this lady, and a dozen company managers throughout the city, read in the gutter press the next morning the terrible news-flash: *"Ghouls Justwanna Halve Foon."*

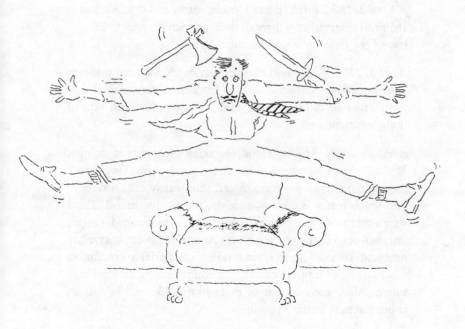

From the Journals of "Woodchuck Charlie" Robinson, Wilderness Guide & Trapper

W.D. SNODGRASS

April 2, 1804. High, fleecy clouds, warm and dry. Ruckus at Iroquois reservation—three of their women pregnant, demand use of the delivery wigwam same night.

April 4, 1804. Light rain and drizzle. Medicine man presents problem of overcrowded tent to Iroquois elders. Tribal customs insist *all* must use tent, and must give birth on skin of their totem animal.

April 7, 1804. Bright, cloudless skies after recent deluge. Medicine man summons women for pow-wow. First wife's totem animal is dog—good. Small skin, easily obtained. Second wife's totem is cow—unwieldy, but readily found. Third wife's totem is hippopotamus. Medicine man enraged—huge, impossible to find, not even North American! Woman says her husband famous hunter, was taken on African expedition where he killed hippopotamus; thereon it became his (and her) totem. Also, she *has* skin of that animal. General uproar in tribe; internal warfare possible.

April 15, 1804. Continual sharp winds, alternate bright sunlight and shade. Iroquois troubles solved. All births successful. Woman of dog totem bears son, woman of cow totem births daughter. Third woman has twins, one male, one female. All doing well. Medicine man reports to tribal elders: *"The squaw of the hippopotamus equals the sum of the squaws of the other two hides."*

True Valu

MARK HARRIS

One of the chiefs of Ifray, whose name was Valu, acquired a great fortune selling shale to the French and Germans. During his late years many people where curious how he would divide his fortune among his heirs, and, although he was well loved by his adherents, many of them it was said were rather pleased when he died, for now they would learn the secret of his last will and testament.

Ifray had married three times. His squaws were named, respectively, in good Ifray arithmetical tradition, Valu-one, Valu-two, and Valu-three. By each of his squaws Valu became the father of sons.

Another chief of Ifray, whose name was Partu, was designated by conventional Ifray procedures to read aloud Valu's will. It was a memorable occasion. Except for a few members of the tribe, absent for reasons of sickness or urgent business, everyone was present for the reading, which occurred on the spacious grassy area adjoining the tribal stables.

Partu assumed the platform, from which in his best voice he directed Valu-one, Valu-two, and Valu-three, the wives of Valu, to seat themselves in the following way before the assembly: Valu-one was to seat herself upon a section of buffalo hide, and Valu-two was to seat herself upon a section of elephant hide, both of which are common enough articles not only in Ifray but throughout the peninsula. Valu-three was to seat herself upon hippopotamus hide which, although by no means rare in Ifray, was less easily obtainable in the shops than buffalo or elephant, or even snake or zebra.

Said Partu once the women were seated, "Now I shall read the instructions of Valu, which are these." One may be certain

that the men and women of Ifray were attentive. Their curiosity about the distribution of Valu's wealth would at last be satisfied. The instructions Partu read were brief and to the point: *"The sons of the squaw on the hippopotamus hide are equal to the sons of the squaws on the other two hides."*

Anyone for Tennyson?

ROBERT TERRALL

*L*ately my name has found its way onto the mailing lists of most of the transplant organizations. I've been willing to give them my signature because I approve of the concept, but as every program has its own card my wallet has been getting almost too bulky to stuff in my pocket. So I've ordered a new card which will cover everything:

"I've signed away eyes, heart and kidneys, so why not take all of me?"

There are lesser difficulties. I'm older now, as aren't we all, and when I go out drinking these days I find that I have a tendency to doze off after only two or three Campari-and-gins. I don't get obstreporous or quarrelsome like some writers I know, merely sleepy. If I've been eating spaghetti with red sauce, for example, I'm careful to move the plate before I lay my head on the table. The bar people don't care for this—I suppose they think it lowers the joint's tone—and sometimes they get a bit nasty. I'm sorry to say that I've been put out a few times. And then, thinking they're being helpful, they complicate matters by calling my wife. I don't want *anybody* called, especially my wife. I just want to be let alone, to find a comfortable doorway and collect my wits, maybe take a brief nap.

So now when I feel my eyelids beginning to close, I prop a card against the ashtray. It may sound peremptory, but it gets results:

"May there be no phoning from this bar, if I'm put out, see?"

Beautiful Princess

FRIEDA ARKIN

*L*ong ago there dwelt a king and queen who were unblessed by children. Magicians, wizards, conjurors and necromancers were daily consulted, and finally they commingled their powers of magic to most happy avail: the queen conceived!

When she was brought to bed with child, those awaiting the birth soon heard through the closed doors: "It's a little princess!" And then a great shout of amazement, and then a tiny wail. There followed a long silence, and then one of the queen's ladies emerged, a kerchief pressed to her eyes. "Such . . . such . . . beauty!" she gasped, and stumbled away.

Such was said to be the beauty of the little princess that to behold her was to render the uninitiated almost senseless. For this reason she was reared in seclusion; it was decreed that none could see her until her wedding day.

Years passed, and kings and princes the world over came to sue for her hand, though they knew that none might witness her beauty until after the wedding vows. They offered wealth, kingdoms, lifelong devotion to this earthborn Aphrodite. One of the princes was chosen.

A thousand guests came to the great luncheon following the ceremony and, the meal finished, waited in heart-pounding expectation as the veiled bride was led in. Passionately the prince plucked the veil from her face and everyone in the room beheld, in utterable shock, a face of such enormous, monstrous ugliness that abruptly every guest became violently ill.

This was the face that shipped a thousand lunches.

Down Under

DONALD HONIG

*W*hile piloting his plane over the Australian outback, Eric Davis suddenly heard his engine begin to cough and sputter. The next thing he knew he was dropping helplessly toward the broad, forbidding expanse of desert beneath him. Petrified, he watched and waited. The Australian earth came rushing up at him as he braced himself for the impending impact. It came, loud and abrupt. The last thing he remembered was being hurled forward, a roaring, grinding sound filling his ears.

When he awakened—he didn't know how many hours later—he was looking into the benign, concerned face of a nun. She asked him how he was.

"Who are you?" Eric asked softly. He was lying in a bed in a small, crudely built but spotless hut.

"I'm Sister Beatrice," she said.

"Where am I?" Eric asked.

"At the home of the Sisters of Mercy. You were found near the wreckage of your plane and brought here."

Eric closed his eyes for a moment, taking a deep breath. "How long was I out there?" he asked. "My throat is parched."

Sister Beatrice handed him a cup. "Drink this," she said.

"What is it?" Eric asked, taking the cup and rising to one elbow.

"It's our tea," Sister Beatrice said, her kindly face allowing a faint smile of pride. "Our own special tea. It is made from the urine and perspiration of the koala."

When Eric looked dubiously into the potion in his cup, Sister Beatrice patted him reassuringly on the arm.

"Drink it," she said. "It is magical. It will help restore your strength."

40

Eric brought the cup to his lips, drank, and then immediately turned his head aside and spat.

"There's all sorts of little particles in it," he said, making a sour face.

"Of course," Sister Beatrice said, brightening. *"The koala tea of Mercy is not strained."*

No Slings, No Arrows

LAWRENCE BLOCK

*D*avid Garrick, the eighteenth-century English actor who made his reputation as Richard III, won even greater renown as Hamlet. Shortly before his first performance in that role, Garrick fell and sustained a fractured tibia. He played the part with a cast on his leg, and won raves. While some gossips hinted that the cast was merely a device to permit his continuing the limp that had served him so well as Richard, theatergoers by and large accepted the performance, limp and all.

Garrick went on to play Hamlet on many other occasions, and of course did not limp in the part once his leg had healed. Other lesser actors, however, borrowed not only his interpretation of the role but the limp that had gone with it. Although there is nothing in the play to suggest that the melancholy Dane ought to limp, several generations of English actors hobbled in the part, and, while the theatrical world today has forgotten this curious bit of business, it survives in that perennial opening night wish: "Break a leg!"

It endures, too, in that show biz bromide: *"You can't make a Hamlet without breaking legs."*

On Bendiner's Tenderheartedness

WILLARD ESPY

A tale the truth of which is guaranteed by the author,
save for the base lie about the intentions of the hero toward
the young maiden.

Bendiner one was as young as any,
And as giddy.
They say he gave the eye to many
A young biddy.
As hounds determine by their snout
Direction,
Bendiner's questing nose sniffed out
Affection.
Yet he too gentle was to slap
A skeeter;
He'd say, "You need your little drap,
Poor creeter!"
At cocktails in a drawing room,
Dimly lighted,
A radiant maiden in full bloom
Once he sighted;
And chatting with this fairy-story
Lass,
He made her the obligatory
Pass.
Of Edna Saint Vincent Millay
And her loves
He murmured, then: "Like hers, today
My heart moves;
"Like hers, my candle may not last

Through the night;
But, ah!—to see it in full blast!—
What a sight!"
The modest maiden backed away—
Shy, unwilling.
Alas! 'twas not Bendiner's day
For a killing.
Behind, low candles on a shelf
Flickered—two.
The nether portion of herself
Near them drew.
Now though she'd left his heart as drear
as autumn,
He could not let her hurt her rear
(Or bottom);
And, quick as mother to defend
The babe she dandles,
Cried, *"Stop! or you will burn your end
At both candles!"*

The Ham Shall Lie Down with the...

RICHARD SCHICKEL

*A*n actor of German descent was stranded far up in a wild country when his touring company went broke. This was in the days when performers were generally regarded as criminals to be shunned, not as celebrities to be shined up to, and he found neither succor nor shelter as pennilessly, pathetically, he wandered the lonesome roads. Finally, however, he came upon a lioness playing with her cubs outside their den.

Assuming his most pitiable air, he approached the matriarch and inquired in the most ingratiating of tones: *"Mother, can you lair a mime?"*

Alas, his accent betrayed his origins, and with a great roar the lioness sprang at him. The terrified thespian barely scuttled away with his life.

"Why did you do that, Mommy?" one of the cubs asked. "He seemed nice."

The mother drew herself up to her full moral height. "What I'm going to say I want you never, ever to forget as long as you live," she growled. *"A hun is the lowest form of roomer."*

A Colorless Story

WILLIAM COLE

I was on my annual autumn wine-buying trip to France, visiting the great vineyards. Having toured the Alsace vineyards, sipping my way through Anjou and Touraine, tippling through St-Emilion, and lurching finally into the Rhone Valley, I found myself at the two-hundred-year old chateau of venerable M. Rachlis, the greatest vintner in France. His production is small but his Burgundies are considered by many to be the rival of the *premiers crus*.

Greeting me, M. Rachlis assured me that this year's grapes were unrivaled. The weather had been perfect, the rainfall just right. "It could be a year like '19 or '59, eh Bill? Now I have something special for you to taste."

With that he took me down the stone stairway leading to the wine cellar. Ducking through the arched entranceway, he led me over to a table on which stood several bottles of newly pressed white wine. He held up one of the bottles for me to examine. White? It was positively colorless!

"Now!" he said. "Try this. It will amaze you!"

He uncorked the bottle with a flourish and poured some in a glass. I sniffed it carefully, then tasted it. No smell, no taste *and* no color!

"Your opinion, Monsieur?" he asked. "Would you purchase some of this?"

"Faugh!" I spit out. *"Albino wine before its time!"*

Is Cape Ann Huge at the Tip? No, Ann Is a Mile of Land!

GEORGE CUOMO

*W*hen novelist Heinrich Böll vacationed on Cape Ann some years back, the resort staff was so awed by Germany's Nobel Prize-winner that among themselves they referred to him, most respectfully, as Der Böll. While there he hosted a number of literary salons, elegant, exclusive affairs where the schnapps flowed freely. Presence was strictly by invitation only, and so great was everyone's desire to be singled out for this honor that those passed over turned churlish and envious.

Upon hearing this, Böll decided to keep the attendance list secret, inviting each guest by a handwritten note discreetly delivered by the resort's chief steward, a trustworthy man whom he swore to silence in the matter.

When the beautiful Swedish film star, Ultima Thole, arrived at the resort, Böll immediately decided to invite her to his next soiree. He learned, however, that she was not only a teetotaler herself but so opposed to the use of alcohol that she refused to attend any function at which it was served.

Böll did not see that as a problem. The next day he wrote her a beautifully embellished invitation, which he entrusted to the faithful steward to deliver. But the poor fellow tumbled down a flight of stairs on his way to Thole's suite and broke his leg. Determined that his task be completed, he asked one of the resort's chambermaids to deliver the note for him. She was a gossipy creature, however, so he was careful to instruct her. *"Do not tell for whom Der Böll asks."* He then handed her the unmarked envelope and confided, *"It's Thole for tea."*

A Rebel Belle

TOM DISCH

Gertrude had vowed to her father, Colonel Ravenal, that even in defeat she would make any sacrifice required of her for the Confederate cause. When the tyrant's brave assassin appeared at their ruined plantation, with the Yankee dogs in hot pursuit, she agreed to her father's strategem.

After his wounds had been bandaged, the handsome young patriot was dressed in Gertrude's warmest traveling frock, and she assumed his clothes *en travestie*. When the two coaches arrived, Colonel Ravenal explained the situation to their fellow conspirators: *"Trudy is Booth, Booth's Trudy. That's all you need to know."*

Through Time and Space with Ferdinand Feghoot

GRENDEL BRIARTON

*I*t was Ferdinand Feghoot who introduced Mozart to Mary Jo Scroggs, who inspired one of his most famous operas.

"Your genius isn't declining," he told the despondent composer. "Opera has become too effete, too pretentious. You need to capture the verve of the lower classes—but of course without any embarrassing complications. I know just the girl, and she lives only two centuries away."

When Mary Jo stepped out of the time shuttle's cabin in her pretty little flour-sack frock, Mozart was instantly smitten. He boasted to everyone in Vienna of her pert little nose, her impertinent breasts, her tiny waist and her pattable bottom. Finally, when it came time for her to return to her Tennessee mountains, "My dear," he cried, "Ferdinand has sworn that you will hear my new work! I could never have done it without you."

And the first question he asked when Ferdinand came back a month later was: "Tell me, what did she think of it?"

"She liked the music," Feghoot reported. "She said it was 'durn near as good a country rock hoedown.' But when I looked at her after final curtain, she was crying."

"*Crying?*" Mozart was stricken. "But *why?*"

"Well," said Ferdinand Feghoot, "you went on so about what a cute shape she had, she jes' reckoned you oughta of called it: *The Figure of Mary Jo.*"

A Spin Around Town

MADELEINE L'ENGLE

A group of acrobats from Pamplona in the Navarre province in northern Spain where invited to the United States. They had never even been to Madrid, let alone a big city like New York before, and were naturally quite excited by it. The producer, who had discovered them while vacationing in the Spanish countryside, wanted the acrobats to enjoy all New York had to offer, so he made certain that they missed nothing. They stayed at a fine midtown hotel, ate at the best restaurants, visited the museums and the Statue of Liberty.

But the acrobats' favorite things in New York were not these passive sight-seeing pleasures. They preferred the action of the rickety wooden roller coaster at Coney Island which provided thrills they only dreamed existed.

The subway ride back to midtown (because of course they eschewed the limo provided by our producer) was even more exhilarating. But the biggest thrill of all came that evening when they were taken to a restaurant which was entered through a revolving door. This was more exciting than either the roller coaster or the subway, and they all crowded in and twirled around and around. Faster, and faster the revolving door spun—until there was a giant pileup and, alas! they were all crushed to death.

The moral of all this is: *You should never put all your Basques in one exit.*

Resting Comfortably

MAX WILK

*P*enelope, oh Penelope! A cat for all seasons—(excepting winter, which so irritated you that you refused to leave the house). And thereby caused us to push you, complaining bitterly as you did, into the frigid white February landscape. When you returned you stared balefully out at me from your safe place by the fire. Oh yes, I blame nobody but myself for the rest of it, the infection, the subsequent illness, the hurry-up trip to Dr. Kalbfus's Veterinary Hospital and, finally, your passing. Despair. Depression. Guilt.

Then, the difficult decision. Bury you? No, no! A free spirit such as you, dear Penny, should be cremated, and when it comes my time to leave, the same for me. So I gave Dr. Kalbfus specific instructions.

The phone rang the next day. *What? Lost?* Impossible! How incredibly careless. *Find her*—don't you understand— this was no ordinary cat! This was a princess!

I paced. I cursed. I considered hiring a lawyer to take that clod of a doctor to court; to have the authorities close down Kalbfus and his gang of white-coated fumblers.

Past six, and another call. "We found her!" they announced. (Ghastly—some idiot had inadvertently consigned her to a garbage pail, but at the last moment, before the dumpster was hauled off, she'd been recovered and, I was reassured, properly cremated.)

Now you, my dear friend, sit safely on the mantelpiece, at the fire you so loved . . . and once again, *a Penny saved is a Penny urned*.

The Man Who Kept Shakespeare in Stitches

BETTE GREENE

*B*ecause Shakespeare was so deeply absorbed during the writing of his tragedies, he put almost impossible strains on his bladder. To make matters even worse, the tiny hooks and eyes that his tailor had placed on his pants slowed down the process considerably. So the playwright demanded that the tailor make larger hooks and eyes.

After a few days of trial, the Bard reported back, "Truly it's speedier these larger hooks and eyes, but still and all, when I'm in a hurry, it's not quick enough. So I want you to redesign my trousers using leather ties."

The tailor did exactly as he was told and Shakespeare jumped into the pants without delay. Exactly one week later, however, the playwright was back at his door. "Truly the leather straps are faster than those hooks and eyes, but even so it's still too slow. So I propose that you throw away the straps and just cut me a little hole."

The tailor bounced to his feet. "You ask for hooks, I give you hooks. You ask for straps, I give you straps. But holes? Holes! You of all people ought to know that *there's no holes, Bard!*"

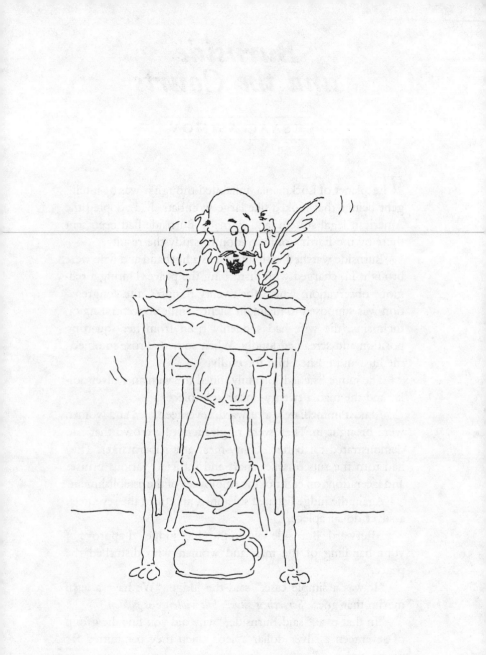

Burnside
and the Courts

ISAAC ASIMOV

*T*he planet of Lockmania, inhabited though it was by intelligent beings that looked like large wombats, had adopted the American legal system, and Barnaby Burnside had been sent there by the Earth Confederation to study the results.

Burnside watched with interest as a husband and wife were brought in, charged with disturbing the peace. During a religious observation, when, for twenty minutes, the congregation was supposed to maintain silence while concentrating on their sins, the wife had suddenly risen from her squatting position and screamed loudly. When someone rose to object, the husband pushed him forcefully.

The judge listened solemnly, fined the woman a silver dollar and the man a twenty-dollar gold piece.

Almost immediately afterward, seventeen men and women were brought in. They were ringleaders of a crowd that had demonstrated for better quality meat at a supermarket. They had torn the supermarket apart and inflicted various bruises and lacerations on eight of the employees of the establishment.

Again the judge listened solemnly, and fined the seventeen a silver dollar apiece.

Afterward, Burnside said to the chief judge, "I approve of your handling of the man and woman who disturbed the peace."

"It was a simple case," said the judge. "We have a legal maxim that goes: *'Screech is silver, but violence is golden.'*"

"In that case," said Burnside, "why did you fine the group of seventeen a silver doliar apiece when they committed far worse violence?"

"Oh, that's another legal maxim," said the judge. *"Every crowd has a silver lining."*

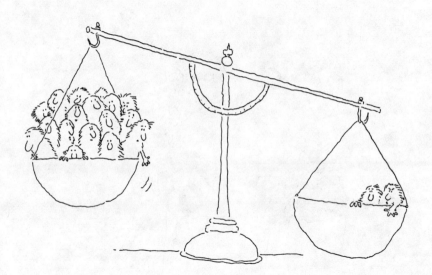

Feghoot with Black Bean Sauce

RICHARD ELMAN

*T*he Chinese Ambassador to the UN invites the diplomatic community of New York to a party at his embassy, a former deluxe motel on the Upper West Side of Manhattan.

Guests are advised to bring swimsuits as they'll be served hot and sour soup from the motel swimming pool.

Vernon Walters, the U.S. Ambassador, formerly of the CIA, asks his aide to telephone and request wonton soup.

The Chinese Ambassador is furious: "General Walters have a hell of a nerve."

"But it's only a change from hot and sour to wonton. Maybe he doesn't want to get his bathing suit all messed up," his aide defends.

"You tell him to go wok his dolly," says the Ambassador. "I do not do wantonness with him."

But then he thinks a minute. "Okay, we will try to oblige on behalf of the Third World."

The night of the party the General arrives and repairs immediately to the pool, which is brimming thick with roilsome black flies.

"What's the meaning of this?" Walters demands.

The Ambassador is summoned and is asked the same question.

He peers at Walters with sly amusement. "You Jewish?"

"Certainly not. Why do you ask?"

"Not me. Shakespeare," says the Ambassador, "has pointed out, as I'm sure you must remember: *'As flies to wonton goys...'*"

Production Values

JOE HALDEMAN

*E*arly in the twenty-first century a Broadway producer named Brian Grendleton Clubfoot IV developed a consuming passion for the science fiction of the previous century. He decided that the contemporary audience, starved for live drama, enervated by dry political wit and onstage copulation, was ripe for adaptations of those fine old tales.

He chose one that had been successful both as novella and cinema: *A Boy and His Dog*, by Harlan Ellison. An added attraction was that Ellison was still alive, and still working in Hollywood.

Ellison agreed to do the stage adaptation, though technology had made the job easier: live actors on Broadway had all been replaced by androids—who required no rehearsal time, never showed up late, and had no union—and so writers had to be programmers as well as artists. Ellison was up to the task, though. He wrote and programmed, and programmed and wrote. B. Grendleton Clubfoot read the *Boy* script as it developed and raved with enthusiasm, heaping praise on Ellison.

But praise was all he heaped. At polite intervals Ellison inquired as to the money that had been promised for the job. B.G. Clubfoot IV always said the check was in the mail, or on his desk, or his secretary had it, or this or that. What a great script, though, Harlan—keep up the good work.

Suspecting that B.G. Clubfoot had no intention of paying, Ellison developed a second script in secret, rather less brilliant than the one he was showing Clubfoot. And sure enough, even on opening night the scurrilous producer had not yet found the cash.

So as the audience assembled, Ellison went backstage and swapped cassettes on the Mark Four Directorbot. Then he took his seat front row center, and settled back with a smile.

With the new script, the play was an utter disaster. Characters from Gasoline Alley coupled with dialogue from Nancy Drew. It was nonsense, but it was *dull* nonsense. The audience fell sound asleep, except for the critics who scribbled feverishly.

Supposed author of the play—Brian Grendleton Clubfoot IV.

During intermission Brian G.C. IV clumped down the stairs to front row and railed and cursed and wept at Harlan, "How could you do this to me? I'm ruined!"

Harlan stroked his white beard and gave the man a pitying smile. "You poor fool. Haven't you figured it out? *All work and no jack makes* Boy *a dull play.*"

Studied Composition

ANNIE DILLARD

A fellow went to Julliard, studied composition. He wanted to be a composer, but after he graduated he saw there was no future in it, so reluctantly he took the only job in music he could find, which was as a singing teacher at a school for retarded children.

He very much liked working with these kids, and after the first few years he had developed a top-notch singing group. This group became famous and toured the country. In city after city, the little kids would sing and the people would applaud and the mayor would have them all over to his house for Coke, ice cream and cake.

Unfortunately after several months of this, the kids started getting fat. Their singing teacher knew they'd lose their popularity if they got fat, so he had to put a stop to it. He began telling the mayors and their hosts wherever they went on tour,

"Look, I know the kids are cute and you want to do something nice for them, but they're getting a bit overweight, so if you want to give them a treat after the concert, give them a Tab, give them an apple, but please, no more ice cream and cake."

Wherever they toured, their hosts agreed to this mild request. And from then on they were known as *The Moron Tab and Apple Choir*.

What I'd Do for Love

DAVID R. SLAVITT

*A*mazingly stupid. And gross. Nevertheless, there was this whaling vessel that sank in a storm, and several members of the crew managed miraculously to survive, hanging onto the gunnels of one of the whale boats. Even more miraculously, they washed up on a deserted island on which they found some coconut palms, and managed to eke out a meager existence there, fishing in the lagoon. They used the whale boat and made nets out of the coconut fiber, and thus were able to keep body and soul together.

It was all share and share alike, except for the second mate who insisted that he was an officer and ought not be required to do the menial jobs of an able seaman. He wouldn't dig latrines, and he wouldn't caulk the whale boat. He thought that was beneath him. Rather than fight about it, the others just gave in.

But then, one day, one of the crew saw a dolphin and got very excited. He built a kind of pen, and he lured the dolphin into the pen, then dove down into the water. He came up shortly and announced that, yes, it was a lady dolphin. He dove back, stayed underwater for a while, and then came up smiling.

The others realized soon enough that he'd figured out how to have sex with the dolphin, and the rest of them wanted to do this too. This was okay with the seaman who'd found the dolphin and captured her—for all of them, that is, except the second mate. Unless he started sharing the menial jobs, he could find his own dolphin. Or he could have sex with the jellyfish and squid in the lagoon.

The second mate objected, but eventually he gave in as they all knew he would. He said what they were all sure he'd say sooner or later: *"I'd caulk a while for a mammal."*

70

Poor Richard

FREDERIK POHL

Dicky Cory, rich as sin,
   Made his fortune out of poultry-raising,
Could find no maiden to give in,
   Went around with all his passions blazing,
Thought his life a total blight,
   Looked on his chicken coops and sadly said,
"No girls for me!"—and, late that night,
   Went home and *put a pullet through his bed*.

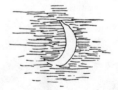

A Stiff Curriculum

X.J. KENNEDY

Deep in a Colorado cave, Professor Horstwessel had founded Troglodyte University, a center of learning impervious to nuclear attack. Its entire faculty consisted of himself, with a single student body. For months all went well—the versatile professor lectured on Dante, relativity, the twelve-tone scale. The neophyte troglodyte, a pale and studious nerd, took notes.

One day Horstwessel made an amazing find. Three stalagmites on the cave's floor were petrified phalluses. A saber-toothed tiger's. A wooly mammoth's. The third, like a foot-thick salami of rock, must be a brontosaurus's.

In front of these stony organs Horstwessel held class. He lectured on this miracle that limewater had wrought. He discoursed on the evolution of sex organs, on the role of the phallus in primitive religion. Rapt, he forgot to break for lunch.

All day long the cave-dwelling student scribbled. But toward five in the afternoon his eyes glazed and his pencil slowed to a halt. "Professor," he muttered, "all this talk about animals' lovelife reminds me that I don't have any. Can't you change your tune?"—"Insubordination!" thundered Horstwessel. "Back to your notes!"

On and on he droned, erecting a theory of penile aesthetics, until at last the student stood up, kicked loose the brontosaurus's phallus, and cracked it over Horstwessel's head.

Hours later, dome throbbing, Horstwessel awoke. He recognized his mistake. *You can't teach a new trog old dicks.*

Psychobabble

CHARLES WEBB

*R*enowned psychiatrist I.M. Looney is appalled by how much trouble American men have talking about their problems. He ascribes the condition to our culture's "relentless optimism" and "unsatisfactory role models."

"Look at boys' heroes," he tells Johnny, Michael, Merv. "Does Superman admit that Lois Lane has hurt his feelings, or that kryptonite scares him? Does Batman worry about the pressures of crime-fighting, or complain that he must hide his true feelings for Robin behind the guise of fatherly mentor?"

To combat this "inauthenticity"—and attack sexism at the same time—Dr. Looney decides to market a series of talking dolls for boys. The dolls will feature the boys' favorite heros, but with one special feature: instead of saying things like, "Hi, I'm Tarzan, King of the Jungle," and yodeling, the heros will talk about their worries, disappointments, insecurities. These Real Hero dolls will tell the truth about their lives!

But these dolls cannot be mere wind up toys. To appeal to today's sophisticated boy, the dolls must embody high technology. Consequently, Dr. Looney contacts Calvin Tek, computer wizard, and sells him on the idea. Soon Cal has the prototypes, complete with prospective prices. The Superman doll ($50) worries for ten minutes straight about his problems with intimacy and his fear of flying. The Spiderman doll ($500) grumbles and groans for a solid hour. For $5,000 the Batman doll complains and crabs for a week.

Dr. Looney is more than satisfied. In fact, he thinks that Batman may be overdoing it. But Calvin, obsessed, keeps working. Six months later, at a price tag of $50,000, he produces a Conan the Barbarian doll which carps and grouses—never once repeating itself—for an entire year.

But even this does not satisfy Cal Tek. He works day and night for another year, and finally finishes his magnum opus, the true Top of the Line Real Hero doll, to sell for a hefty $500,000. He wires Dr. Looney the good news: *"Hurrah! The Tarzan Gripes Forever!"*

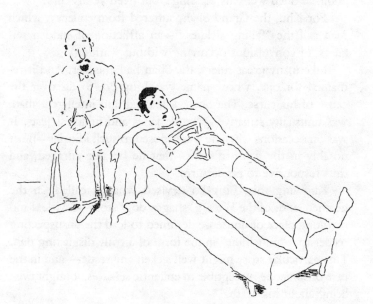

The Shaggy Dog Bite

ROBERT BLOCH

*I*n all the world no man was more blessed than Khu, the Grand Shan of Tartary—nor more cursed.

None exceeded him in power or riches, the breadth of his domain, the virtues of his wife, and the vices of his concubines. Such were his blessings, but heed ye his curse.

For Khu, the Grand Shan, suffered from epilepsy, which men call the "falling sickness"—an affliction of sudden seizures, of convulsions occurring without warning.

Like many great rulers, the Shan had enemies. And it remained for one, whose name was Ling-Po, to discover the cause of his curse. The Shan, a learned and intelligent man, was unusually sensitive to crude japes and mindless jests. It was on occasions when he was exposed to such idiocies—most notably in the form of puns—that he became enraged, and thus responsive to his seizures.

Knowing this, Ling-Po devised what is called, in the heathen lands of the West, a "shaggy dog" story—a witless and revolting piece of nonsense designed to lead the unsuspecting reader to a "punchline" in the form of a truly disgusting pun. This particular story might well sicken any reader—and in the case of someone susceptible to epileptic seizures, it might even bring about his death.

Ling-Po inscribed his work on a scroll of parchment inserted in a golden tube, and personally presented it to the Shan as a birthday gift from an anonymous admirer.

Presently it came to pass that the Shan unrolled the scroll. Ling-Po waited, his heart pounding in uncertainty as the Shan began to read. Would the Shan indeed experience an epileptic seizure when he came upon the filthy pun at the end?

The reading concluded, and for a moment Ling-Po waited, wondering if he had failed. But he need not have worried, once the pun was read. For it was *then that the fit hit the Shan*.

A Jonathan Swifty

BROCK BROWER

*W*hen Jonathan Swift died on October 19, 1745, he left the bulk of his fortune to the building and endowment of an insane asylum. "A hospital large enough for the reception of as many lunatics and idiots as the annual income . . . shall be sufficient to maintain." He wished the asylum to be called St. Patrick's Hospital, but it is usually referred to as Swift's—who himself died mad. *Did Swift so hate the world that he left his only begotten sum to shame it?*

Routine Teuton

PETER STRAUB

A German-born boy named Carabaggio, feeling himself conspicuous because of his Italian ancestry, tries for some time to become the perfect German. At the University of Munich he joins the dueling team, goes drinking in the Bierstubes with his classmates, and even dyes his hair a shade blonder. When he graduates he makes his way to Paris where, impulsively, he tries to steal a brass miniature of the Eiffel Tower. He is arrested and given the choice of leaving France or going to jail. An easy decision.

He takes the first boat for New York and when he arrives he goes immediately to the RCA Building, bursts into General Sarnoff's office and demands a job. Sarnoff likes his style and tells him he can have a job as a strikebreaker. The boy accepts, but as soon as the strike is over, he is out of work again.

Utilizing his engineering degree, he finds employment in a sonar equipment factory owned by a Mr. Harris. He works hard, perfects his English, and several years later gets a job as a disc jockey on a program called "Rock Time." Alas, one morning on the way to work he is struck by a taxi and killed.

His epitaph reads as follows:

He was a routine Teuton, Eiffel-lootin', Sarnoff goon from Harris Sonar, Rock-Time Carabaggio.

Courtesy of Paul Desmond

The Secret Ingredient of the Wee Intangible Essence Burger

TOM CLARK

*A*n East Coast weekly magazine famous for its dogged pursuit of fact dispatched a reporter to cover the Loch Kibble Hamburger Festival. The world's great cooks, the reporter was told, converge annually on this remote Scottish moor to compete for the international burger-cooking championship.

"Why's the thing held in Scotland, for god's sake?" the reporter asked.

"Used to be in Brooklyn," his editor said. "But some guy who lives in Loch Kibble's won it the last twenty-two years. Finally they just moved it there. Not long after the Dodgers left, that happened—and he's still going strong."

The reporter was instructed to interview the world champion, Angus McDonald of Loch Kibble.

He flew to Scotland, found his way to Loch Kibble, and watched from under an umbrella at grillside as McDonald, a huge kilted man in a white regulation cook's apron several sizes too small for him, steamed uncontested through the compulsory events and then into his specialty, the Wee Intangible Essence Burger. He'd won the championship before his last burger was even off the grill.

After the event the reporter approached the great hamburger chef for an interview. McDonald politely declined. The reporter pressed, McDonald refused and departed. Another writer on hand for the event commiserated, "It's a shame, mate, but you've come all this way over the water for nothing. Angus McDonald will *never* reveal the ingredients of his Wee Intangible Essence Burger, and that's that."

The reporter persisted. After the award ceremony, he followed McDonald home. Hiding behind a clump of gorse, he watched the great cook reemerge, still in his kilt, carrying golf clubs.

McDonald sauntered to the local course, where he teed off through the heavy fog. As dusk came on, other players left the course. Finally McDonald was alone. With the reporter watching from deep in the heather, the great burger chef looked around, then reached under his kilt and pulled out what looked like a gamebag on a stick. He began running across the moor, swiping at the fog, scooping up bagfuls of atmosphere.

The reporter stepped forward and confronted the champion. "I've been watching you, McDonald," the reporter said. "I think I've discovered the secret of your Wee Intangible Essence Burger."

McDonald peered down at him. "And what might that be, laddie?"

The reporter pointed down at the gamebag in McDonald's hand. "The golf is just a cover. You've been running around this moor in this fog catching your secret ingredient."

The great Scottish champion's poker face collapsed into a caught-in-the-act grin that was almost sheepish. Then he roared out with laughter.

"Well, they've found me out at last! Aye, laddie, you're right—*it's all mist for the grill!*"

The Fox Who Loved Ice Cream

HANNAH GREEN

*O*nce upon a time there was a fox who loved ice cream. He traveled all over his neck of the woods dining in restaurants and ordering ice cream for dessert. He tried all the flavors and he loved them all because they were *all* ice cream. At length he decided to go abroad, to travel in France where ice cream is called *glace*.

He booked his passage on a fine old ship and set sail from New York to Le Havre. He went straight to the restaurant at the train station where he believed he saw General Eisenhower dining with his dog. It did not matter that General Eisenhower had died some time before, for the fox believed in immortality, and he thought that France was heaven. General Eisenhower was reading a book on *aquarelle* while his dog observed the passing scene. The fox thought the ice cream was heavenly.

Now as he traveled through the country, the fox stopped each night at a hotel and dressed for dinner in his white tie and tails so that he had three tails in all — the two swallowtails of his suit and his own foxtail. He was withal a most handsome fox. A bit red, perhaps, but he made up for this fault by his nice smile and his overall agreeable disposition. Occasionally he barked in French, but he never bit.

The food and the dishes of the various regions were all he had been told they would be, but his favorite part of the meal came when the waiter or waitress asked him what he wanted for dessert and he chose *"Glace!"* Then the waiter had to recite the various *parfums* there were for him to choose from—

vanille, chocolat, cafe, pistache, or *mystere.* The fox loved to listen to this recitation of flavors, and then with delight would choose the one that had caught his fancy for that evening.

At length he reached a strange wild country where the River Rhone flows into the sea. There were wild white horses in the flat salt marshes, and wild bulls. There were flamingos standing in the lagoons and flying in the sky with a pink light glowing through them. There was a wild wind, too, called the mistral, and an old church called Les Saintes Maries de la Mer where the gypsies came to worship their Saint Sara in a crypt hot with candle flames.

On this night when the fox came to dinner in his white tie and tails there was a lovely waitress, young and gentle and shy. She was very pale of skin but with rosy cheeks. It was she who, when he had finished dining on his choice of cheeses, recited to the fox the flavors of the ice cream. The fox made her do it twice just to listen to her sweet voice saying, *"Vanille, chocolat, cafe, pistache, mystere."* The fox chose *mystere.* There was no one in the hotel dining room except for himself and the young waitress. Outside in the winter night the stars were very bright.

The fox began to eat his *mystere.* But in the very first bite he detected something hard, something out of place, something that did not seem to want to be chewed. Very neatly he removed it from his mouth. He held it up to the little light on his table, and he saw it was a pearl. He stared at it, for it glowed in the light like a little moon and it shimmered with rose and violet and blue and green in a pearly way. The waitress came over to his table. "Is there anything the matter, sir," she said. The fox was still looking at the pearl. Then he looked up at her and he saw that her skin was as lovely as that of the pearl. The fox was overcome with shyness. He looked down at the pearl. *"What is a nice pearl like you doing in a glace like this?"* he asked.

The fox failed to finish his *mystere.* He left ten francs on the table along with the little pearl—though he wasn't sure that she would see it. As he went to bed that night, for the first time in his life, he realized that he was alone.

The image shows a movie clapperboard reading "MR ED Takes A Powder / TAKE 2"

Animal Rights

WALTER REDFERN

John Dough, the archetypal adman, was desperate for a new idea to sell his product. It was an itching powder for a novelty firm, so you can see he had problems.

The people he engaged let him down in various ways: their laughter was artificial, or they looked excruciated instead of tickled to death. So he decided to switch to animals, who would also come cheaper.

But a chimp went hysterical; the hyena was already over the top before they got started. "What about a horse?" he thought. "Funnybone Itching-Powder would make a horse laugh!" He'd have to work on the slogan, but it had possibilities.

He put ads in the specialty animal press. Among the dozens of replies, he picked a Barbary steed of surpassing beauty. When it and master arrived, Dough was amazed to discover that the horse could also talk, though aristocratically it never finished its sentences. No use exploiting this fantastic ability then. Dough resolved to ask it to whinny throughout the take. But the steed had not only beauty and the gift of speech, but also a sharp business brain. It answered, in its no-nonsense, sawn-off way: *"If you want me to neigh through the pose, you'll have to. . ."*

Fish Story

ROBERT CANTWELL

A few years ago it was fashionable in the scientific community to imagine that some animals—dolphins, in this case—had an intelligence comparable to or perhaps even greater than human beings. Dolphins, it seems, have a kind of language, a strange, high-pitched sort of screech, which when slowed down electronically to less than half its normal rate reveals something like words and sentences that mimic the sounds of the workers around them.

Two scientists had secured a grant from a major university to study this phenomenon, and had set up a complicated laboratory in the expectation of spending at least ten years on the project. Contrary to their original expectations, the biologists soon realized the dolphins seemed to flourish on a fairly steady diet of gull meat. This unlikely food not only contributed to their general good health, but actually seemed to extend the life spans of the mammals well beyond their usual expectancy. And, as is typical in good scientific work, this casual discovery came to occupy more and more of the biologists' attention, until it became as important as their work on language—in fact, to a few on the staff it seemed *more* important. Perhaps there was something in the gull meat, some enzyme or something, that might expand the *human* life span and retard the aging process.

But funds for the experiment were abruptly cut off with a change in the university administration. Too late, however, to cool the ardor of a few young investigators who were now on the track, they thought, of that ever elusive object, eternal life. They chose to carry on their work covertly, using the dolphins in the local zoo, actually a wild animal park which included rides and water shows as well as animals in nature-like settings.

To feed these animals their gull meat fare, it was necessary to enter the park in secret, at night, not through the main gate of course, which was heavily guarded and equipped with electronic surveillance devices, but through a hidden gap in the park fence. This subterfuge required a harrowing creep through a grassy area populated by a pride of lions. After a few failed attempts, however—three people lost their nerve, and turned back—a solution was finally arrived at: it was to cross the area at dusk, just after the lions had been fed their raw meat, at which time they were sluggish and often actually asleep.

The experiment was able to continue in this way for several weeks, and began to assume something like its original form. The gull meat was administered and appropriate measurements taken, tests on the animals conducted all at night. However, the experiment abruptly ended one night at dusk, when two scientists were ignominiously arrested as they entered the dolphin shed—arrested not for trespassing, as they first supposed, but for a much more severe crime under the Mann Act: *Transporting gulls over sated lions for immortal porpoises.*

An Artful Decision

WILLIAM THOMPSON

*T*he ad exec was meeting with the new client—the owner of the most successful and prestigious art gallery in the world. Dozens of sixteenth- to eighteenth-century paintings had been displayed and exchanged hands at astonishing prices. With success came expansion, and the gallery owner was looking for the right agency to handle his projected new ad budget.

The campaign was to be elegant, tasteful, and focused at the well-heeled, discriminating buyer who wanted to view or own genuine old masters.

For weeks our ad exec labored over the campaign. It was masterful; it was creative; it was painstakingly thought out. It was targeted exactly to the market as described. Our exec knew he had a winner.

In keeping with the detail keynoting every step of the ad campaign, the exec dressed carefully for the meeting which would unveil it: the white shirt and dark blue suit. He surveyed his ties—refined and tasteful, he thought. He chose a silk polka-dot — restrained and understated but undeniably elegant.

The exec proceeded to the presentation more sure of himself than ever before. This one could not fail.

But it did. The gallery owner sat stonily viewing the outlined ad campaign. From the very first, the exec sensed some wave of disapproval from the gallery owner. What could have gone wrong?

When he heard that the account had gone to his chief competition, he was so crestfallen that he went to the gallery owner to find out what had happened.

"Please," he said, "tell me what made you choose the other agency."

"Your campaign was brilliant," the gallery owner answered sadly, "and would have done honor to my name and my profession and the old world artists I deal in. It was much better than your competition."

"But, if you felt that way, why didn't you choose me for your ad exec?" He was stupefied.

"It was your tie."

"My tie? But I chose that polka-dot especially."

"But you chose it more in Seurat than in Ingres!"

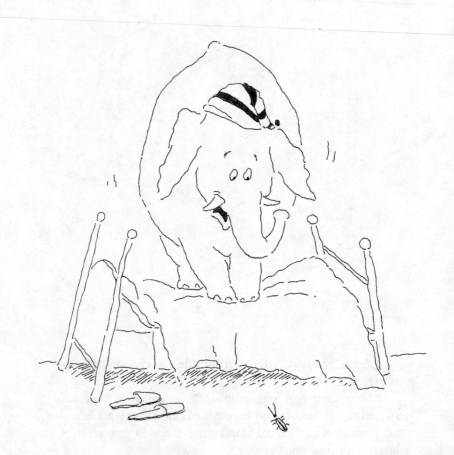

Flowers for Pachyderm

MARK STRAND

As Franz Kafka awoke one morning from uneasy dreams, he found himself transformed into a raging bull elephant. He charged around his room with his trunk sticking straight up making loud trumpeting noises. The picture of the lady in furs came crashing down, the vase of anemones tipped over. Suddenly afraid that his family might discover him, Franz stuck his enormous head out of the window overlooking the courtyard. But it was too late. His parents and sisters had already been awakened by the racket, and rushed into his room. All of them gasped simultaneously as they stared at the great bulk of Franz's rump. Then Franz pulled his head and turned toward them, looking sheepish. Finally, after an awkward couple of minutes in which no one spoke, Franz's mother went over and rested her cheek against his trunk and said, "Are you ill, dear?" Franz let loose a blood curdling blast, and his mother slipped to the floor. Franz's father was about to help her but noticed the anemones tipped over on the table. He picked them up and threw them out the window, saying, *"With Franz like this, who needs anemones?"*

A Baseball Groaner

W.P. KINSELLA

*I*n the early years of the century there were vaudeville-like entertainers who followed the minor league baseball circuits, putting on shows before and after games, sometimes even between innings. One act billed itself as "G. Barrer, Dog Trainer." Barrer had a brilliant dog named Rover who danced, leapt through flaming hoops and, standing on his hind legs, played first base, catching a rubber ball in his teeth, always keeping one foot on the bag.

Barrer, the dog trainer, owned a second dog, an understudy, that was not very smart; its name had originally been Rover, so it was called, ironically, Clever Rover. One night, just before showtime, Rover disappeared. Barrer was forced to use the understudy, a dog that fell over when he danced, singed his fur as he knocked over the flaming hoops, and caught only about one of every four balls lobbed at him.

"The dog is incompetent!" cried Barrer to his assistant. "Find Rover and get him in here right now!"

The assistant replied, "Yo! G. Barrer, I'll do my best. But until then, *it's Clever Rover till it's Rover*."

Armor, Amour

JOEL OPPENHEIMER

*I*n the olden days Prague, a then modern and enlightened city in the midst of barbarian Teutonic types, was a target for any petty warlord who could raise an army.

One of the most serious attacks was mounted in 1330 when several German princes put the city under siege. The King of Prague used diplomacy, strategy, and the city's stout walls to keep the enemy at bay, but still the siege held and the situation was getting desperate.

Finally, the King decided to fall back on the time-honored tradition of trial by individual combat, and challenged the highest-ranking German prince to a joust. The German prince was noted for his fighting ability, while the King had distinguished himself primarily by humanistic studies, so this seemed a terrible mismatch, and one that would lead to the fall of Prague.

But the King had a secret weapon, or rather, defense—his studies had led to the development of a new sort of armor. He was sure that his discovery would give him more protection and more flexibility, so that he would be able to overcome his opponent, who would be encumbered by rigid, plated armor.

The great day arrived and both heroes rode out for the joust. The people of Prague watched from their city's walls, with the Queen in the midst of them. There was great trepidation, of course, and it was added to by the fact that both men were of about the same height, and both rode black horses. In the dust raised by the battle, one figure could be seen moving swiftly and surely, while the other seemed to lumber about, always a second too late, or an inch too short. The dust obscured the heroes' colors, but the Queen raised a shout as the slower figure fell with a great clattering of his plated armor.

"But how do you know we've won?" asked the anxious townfolk.

"I've told you and told you," said the Queen. *"The Czech is in the mail!"*

A Conventional Approach

JAMES CHARLTON

*P*ercy Shelley was despondent. After banging out pamphlets and poems, odes and dramas with ease he had suddenly run up against that which all poets fear more than editorial rejection—writer's block. No matter how hard he tried, nothing came. Page after page of jibberish went into the basket.

Pacing the streets of Oxford one morning he encountered his good friend Keats. Keats was in fine spirits but soon became solicitous when he heard the poet's plight.

"The very thing happened to me last year," said Keats. "Upon the advice of a friend I visited a small religious retreat, Mount St. Michaela, off the coast of Cornwall. It is run by an order of nuns and there is nothing to do but listen to the surf and the gulls. In no time at all I was afire to put pen to paper."

"Then I shall do it," vowed Shelley, and he hurried off to make arrangements.

Three days later, after a long, dusty and tiring coach ride, he soon arrived in the small coastal village across from the nunnery, and there he hired a skiff to take him over to the island three miles distant. A wind was coming up and the sun was setting as the fisherman methodically pulled the oars, drawing the boat ever nearer. The waves grew angrier but finally the boat scraped alongside a rock and Shelley jumped ashore. Scrambling up the stone steps, he made his way to the front door of the convent and pounded on the heavy wood. Soon a small window opened and a young woman peered out.

"I'm Percy Bysshe Shelley and I've come to stay here awhile. Please let me in."

"I'm only a novitiate," a small voice answered. "Mother Superior has retired for the night and only if I have her signature can I allow you admittance."

"But a storm is coming up and the boat has gone back to the village," pleaded the poet. "Surely you can authorize it yourself."

"I'm very sorry," answered the young sister. "You have to *wait till the nun signs, Shelley*."

Gustatory Notes From All Over

DONALD E. WESTLAKE

A rare delicacy is sautéed *sloth à la Dortmunder*. Using the middle toe of the great Australian three-toed sloth—the only edible part of that large, furry, indolent creature—the careful chef debones it, pounds it as with veal, and sautées it briefly over a hot flame with shallots, carrot circles, and just a touch of Tobasco. Prepared in this fashion, sloth is an excellent main course, not unlike alligator in texture and taste.

Many people are under the false impression that sloth does not make a good meal, but this is because they've eaten it improperly prepared. It can only be sautéed, *à la Dortmunder*, a fact ill-appreciated in culinary circles. *Too many cooks broil the sloth*.

The original sayings, mottos, quotations,
aphorisms, *pensées,* and adages before being emended by
our contributors:

Stephen King
Read any good books lately? (saying)

Donald Hall
Read a good book. (saying)

John D. MacDonald
A rolling stone gathers no moss. (Maxim 524 by Publilius Syrus)

Roy Blount Jr.
There are no atheists in foxholes. (from a 1942 field sermon by
Chaplain William Thomas Cummings)

William Eastlake
There are no atheists in foxholes. (from a 1942 sermon by
Chaplain William Thomas Cummings)
Hollywood doesn't make good pictures any more. (saying)

George Garrett
If you can't stand the heat, get out of the kitchen. (expression
coined by Harry Truman)
Nice guys finish last. (quotation attributed to Leo Durocher)

Anne Bernays
All the News That's Fit to Print. (motto of the New York
Times)

Stephen Birmingham
It's a Long, Long Way to Tipperary. (song title, lyrics by
Harry Williams)

Elizabeth Tallent
Girls Just Want to Have Fun. (song title)

W.D. Snodgrass
The square of the hypotenuse is equal to the sum of the squares of the other two sides. (Pythagorean theorem)

Mark Harris
The square of the hypotenuse is equal to the sum of the squares of the other two sides. (Pythagorean theorem)

Robert Terrall
And may there be no moaning of the bar,
When I put out to sea . . . (from the poem *Crossing the Bar* by Alfred, Lord Tennyson)

Frieda Arkin
Was this the face that launched a thousand ships? (from *The Tragical History of Dr. Faustus* by Christopher Marlowe)

Donald Honig
The quality of mercy is not strained. (from *The Merchant of Venice* by William Shakespeare)

Lawrence Block
You can't make an omelette without breaking eggs. (French proverb)

Willard Espy
My candle burns at both ends;
It will not last the night. (from the poem *A Few Figs From Thistles* by Edna St. Vincent Millay)

Richard Schickel
Brother, can you spare a dime? (Depression expression)
A pun is the lowest form of humor. (saying)

William Cole
I'll buy no wine before its time. (slightly fractured slogan of the Gallo Vineyards)

George Cuomo
No man is an island.
Never send to know for whom the bell tolls; it tolls for thee. (from
Devotions upon Emergent Occasions by John Donne)

Tom Disch
"Beauty is truth, truth beauty,"—that is all
Ye know on earth, and all ye need to know. (from the poem *Ode
on a Grecian Urn* by John Keats)

Grendal Briarton
The Marriage of Figaro. (opera by Wolfgang Amadeus Mozart)

Madeleine L'Engle
'Tis the part of a wise man to keep himself today for tomorrow,
And not venture all his eggs in one basket. (from *Don Quixote* by
Miguel de Cervantes)

Max Wilk
A penny saved is a penny earned. (maxim)

Bette Greene
There are no holds barred. (saying)

Isaac Asimov
"Speech is silver, silence is golden." (quotation translated from the
Swiss by Thomas Carlisle)
Look for the silver lining. (song title, lyrics by B.G. DaSilva)

Richard Elman
As flies to wanton boys . . . (from *King Lear* by William
Shakespeare)

Joe Haldeman
All work and no play makes Jack a dull boy. (from *Proverbs* by
James Howell)

Annie Dillard
The Mormon Tabernacle Choir (Utah singing group)

David Slavitt
I'd walk a mile for a Camel. (cigarette advertising slogan)

Frederik Pohl
Put a bullet through his head. (from the poem *Richard Cory* by
Edwin Arlington Robinson)

X.J. Kennedy
You can't teach an old dog new tricks. (old saw)

Charles Webb
The Stars and Stripes Forever. (march by John Phillip Sousa)

Robert Bloch
When the shit hits the fan. (saying)

Brock Brower
*God so loved the world, that he gave his only begotten Son, that
whosoever believeth in him should not perish, but have everlasting
light. (from The Gospel According to St. John)*

Peter Straub
*He's a rootin'-tootin', high-falutin', son of a gun from Arizona,
Ragtime Cowboy Joe.* (from the song *Ragtime Cowboy Joe* by
Maurice Abrahams, Grant Clarke, and Lewis F. Muir)

Tom Clark
It's all grist for the mill. (bromide)

Hannah Green
What's a nice girl like you doing in a place like this? (pickup line)

Walter Redfern
You'll have to pay through the nose. (saying)

Robert Cantwell
Transporting girls across state lines for immoral purposes. (the
Mann Act)

William Thompson
A countenance more in sorrow than in anger. (from *Hamlet* by William Shakespeare)

Mark Strand
With friends like these, who needs enemies? (saying)

W.P. Kinsella
It's never over till it's over. (quotation attributed to Yogi Berra)

joel oppenheimer
The check is in the mail. (saying)

James Charlton
Wait Till the Sun Shines, Nellie. (song title)

Donald E. Westlake
Too many cooks spoil the broth. (saying)

Frieda Arkin's short stories and poetry have been published by a number of literary magazines, including the *Yale Review* and the *Kenyon Review*, and her several books include *The Dorp*. She lives in Essex, Massachusetts.

Isaac Asimov has published 338 books on every conceivable subject and every title is still in print. Mr. Asimov lives in New York City.

Anne Bernays has written seven novels, among them *The Address Book* and *Growing Up Rich*. Her work has appeared in *New Republic* and *Sports Illustrated* among others. A talented singer as well, she is a member of the Cambridge Chorale.

Stephen Birmingham is the author of more than twenty books of fiction and non-fiction, including *Our Crowd, The Auerbach Will* and the best-selling *The LeBaron Secret*. He lives in Mount Adams, Ohio.

Robert Bloch has been writing psychological suspense and screenplays for forty years. His work, which includes the novel *Psycho*, has won such prizes as the Hugo, Edgar and Nebula awards. He lives in Los Angeles.

Lawrence Block's most recent novel is *When the Sacred Gin Mill Closes*. He has received numerous awards for his novels, including the Edgar Allen Poe Award. Mr. Block lives in Ft. Meyers Beach, Florida.

Roy Blount, Jr., is an essayist and playwright whose work has appeared in dozens of magazines. His latest collection of essays is *Not Exactly What I Had In Mind*. Mr. Blount lives in Mill River, Massachusetts.

Reginald Bretnor's work has appeared in *Harper's* and *Esquire*, and he contributed the article on science fiction in the *Encyclopedia Brittanica*. He is the author of *Decisive Warfare* and other books of military theory, a number of novels, stories, and under the pseudonym Grendal Briarton is the creator of Ferdinand Feghoot. Mr. Bretnor lives in Medford, Oregon.

Brock Brower's work has appeared in *Esquire, American Scholar* and the New York *Times Magazine* and his books include *Other Loyalties: Politics of Personality* and *The Late Great Creature*. A former Rhodes Scholar, he now lives in Princeton, New Jersey.

Robert Cantwell is the author of *Bluegrass Breakdown* and is currently at work on a book about the folk revival for the Smithsonian. His essays have appeared in *The Atlantic* and the *Kenyon Review*. Mr. Cantwell lives in Gambier, Ohio.

James Charlton was an editorial director at several publishing houses in New York, and has ten books published on subjects ranging from croquet to hand gestures. He lives in Greenwich Village, five blocks from where he was born.

Tom Clark is a poet, biographer of Jack Kerouac and novelist whose latest work is *The Exile of Celine*. He has received writing grants from the Rockefeller and Guggenheim Foundations and the National Endowment for the Arts. He lives in Santa Barbara, California.

William Cole has written the "Trade Winds" column for *Saturday Review* for ten years and has published more than sixty books. His poetry has appeared in many magazines and collections, and one poem, *What a Friend We Have in Cheeses*, has appeared in five anthologies. Mr. Cole lives in New York City.

George Cuomo is a novelist and short story writer, and his works include *Among Thieves* and *Family Honor*. Mr. Cuomo teaches at the University of Massachusetts and is the recipient of both Guggenheim and National Endowment for the Arts fellowships.

Annie Dillard won the 1974 Pulitzer Prize for her book *Pilgrim at Tinker Creek*. Recent publications include *Encounters with Chinese Writers* and *Teaching a Stone to Talk*. Ms. Dillard lives in Middletown, Connecticut.

Tom Disch is a science fiction writer whose stories have appeared in such publications as *Omni, Playboy* and the *Paris Review*. He won the 1980 John W. Campbell Memorial Award for *On The Wings of Song*. His latest work is a children's book entitled *The Brave Little Toaster*. Mr. Disch lives in New York City.

William Eastlake is a novelist, short story writer, poet and screenwriter whose work has appeared in more than forty anthologies and textbooks. He served as a correspondent in Vietnam for *The Nation* magazine and now lives in Bisbee, Arizona.

Richard Elman is a novelist and short story writer whose work has appeared in *The Nation, The New Yorker* and *Geo*. His work includes *The Menu Cyphers*, and he received the 1984 PEN/NEA award for short fiction. He lives in New York City.

Willard Espy is the author of numerous books including the best-selling *An Almanac of Words at Play* and *Have a Word on Me*. He and his wife Louise commute between their homes in New York City and Oysterville, Washington.

George Garrett is the author of five novels, including *Death of the Fox,* numerous volumes of poetry and short story collections, several plays, and three screenplays, including *Frankenstein Meets the Space Monster* (cowriter). He is currently the Hoyns Professor of Creative Writing at the University of Virginia.

Hannah Green is a novelist whose work includes the best-seller *I Never Promised You a Rose Garden*. Ms. Green lives in New York City.

Bette Greene has written a number of novels, including *Them That Glitter and Them That Don't* and *Summer of my German Soldier*, a National Book Award finalist and screenplay which she cowrote. Ms. Greene lives in Brookline, Massachusetts.

Joe Haldeman is a science fiction novelist and short story writer. His book *The Forever War* won the Hugo Award and his latest novel, *Dealing in Futures*, is published by Viking. Mr. Haldeman is on the faculty of M.I.T.

Donald Hall is a poet and essayist, and has published more than sixty books. His first play, *The Bone Ring*, was produced off-Broadway in February 1986. He lives in Wilmot, New Hampshire.

Mark Harris is a novelist, essayist and screenwriter. He is perhaps best known for his celebrated novel *Bang the Drum Slowly*, for which he subsequently wrote the screenplay. Mr. Harris is a professor of English at Arizona State University.

Donald Honig's latest book is *Baseball America*. He has written forty-nine other books, both fiction and non-fiction, and his shorter pieces have been published in numerous magazines. He lives in Cromwell, Connecticut.

X.J. Kennedy has written six books of poetry, five children's books, and numerous college poetry texts. He received the 1985 Los Angeles *Times* Book Award for *Cross Ties*, and his latest book is *Brats*, a nonsense collection for children.

Stephen King is the acknowledged master of the horror-suspense genre of fiction. He is also an actor, screenwriter and director, and lives in Bangor, Maine.

W.P. Kinsella is the author of twelve books, including *Shoeless Joe* and *The Iowa Baseball Confederacy*. He lives in Toronto, Canada.

Madeleine L'Engle is the author of thirty-five books of poetry, drama, fantasy and non-fiction. She received the Newberry Medal for her celebrated novel *A Wrinkle in Time*, and has won the American Book Award. Ms. L'Engle is married to actor Hugh Franklin, and lives in New York City.

John D. MacDonald is a novelist whose Travis McGee mysteries have won him millions of fans the world over. His latest best-seller is *The Lonely Silver Rain*. Mr. MacDonald lives in Sarasota, Florida.

joel oppenheimer is a poet and writer whose work includes *The Wrong Season* and *New Spaces*. He was a regular columnist for the *Village Voice*, and now his column appears in the *New Hampshire Times*. He is on the faculty of New England College and lives in Henniker, New Hampshire.

Frederik Pohl has written hundreds of science fiction novels and short stories, and has won virtually every award, including the Hugo and Nebula awards. Mr. Pohl lives in Palatine, Illinois.

Walter Redfern is the author of one novel and a number of scholarly books, including the estimable *Puns*. He is a professor of French at Reading University in England.

Richard Schickel is a film critic for *Time* magazine and the author of many books, including *D.W. Griffith: An American Life*, and *Intimate Strangers*. He lives in New York City.

David Slavitt has published more than thirty-five books of fiction and non-fiction. He received the 1985 Pennsylvania Arts Council Award in Fiction and lives in Philadelphia. He is a lecturer in English at Columbia University.

W.D. Snodgrass is a poet and playwright whose published works include *Remains, In Radical Pursuit* and *Heart's Needle*, for which he won the Pulitzer Prize. Mr. Snodgrass lives in Erieville, New York.

Mark Strand is a poet and writer whose work has appeared in *The New Yorker, Anteus* and *Vogue*. His *Selected Poems* was published by Atheneum. Mr. Strand lives in Salt Lake City.

Peter Straub is a poet and novelist whose works include the best-sellers *Ghost Story* and *Floating Dragon*. Mr. Straub lives in New York City and Greens Farms, Connecticut.

Elizabeth Tallent is a novelist (*Museum Pieces*) and short-story writer. Much of her work has appeared in *The New Yorker, Esquire* and the *Paris Review*. She lives in Espanola, New Mexico.

Robert Terrall is the author of some fifty novels, several of them under his own name, many more under various pseudonyms, most notably, Brett Halliday. Under the latter he has written twenty-four Mike Shayne mysteries, and his latest novel is *Wrap it in Flags*. Mr. Terrall lives in Sharon, Connecticut.

William Thompson is a successful editor who has worked on dozens of best-sellers. He has written one book that was not a best-seller. He lives in New York City.

Charles Webb is a novelist and non-fiction writer whose work includes *The Graduate*. He lives in Los Angeles.

Donald Westlake has written some thirty books and has won the Edgar Allan Poe Award. He lives in New York City.

Max Wilk is a film writer, Emmy-award-winning television writer and novelist with eighteen books published. His latest books are *And Did You Once See Sidney Plain* and *A Tough Act to Follow*. Mr. Wilk lives in Westport, Connecticut.

BRED ANY GOOD ROOKS LATELY?
was designed by Hudson Studio,
Ossining, New York
and produced by James Charlton Associates,
New York, New York